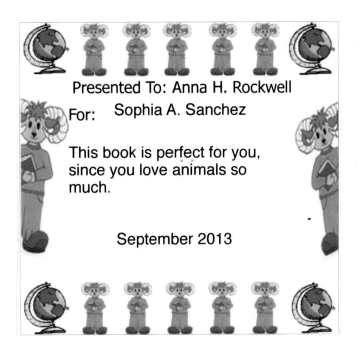

Presented To: Anna H. Rockwell

For: Sophia A. Sanchez

This book is perfect for you,
since you love animals so
much.

September 2013

Rockwell Media Center
Whittlesey Drive
Bethel, CT 06801

# Learn to Draw
# AMAZING ANIMALS

www.av2books.com

AV² provides enriched content that supplements and complements this book. Weigl's AV² books strive to create inspired learning and engage young minds in a total learning experience.

## Your AV² Media Enhanced books come alive with...

**Audio**
Listen to sections of the book read aloud.

**Key Words**
Study vocabulary, and complete a matching word activity.

**Video**
Watch informative video clips.

**Quizzes**
Test your knowledge.

**Embedded Weblinks**
Gain additional information for research.

**Slide Show**
View images and captions, and prepare a presentation.

**Try This!**
Complete activities and hands-on experiments.

**... and much, much more!**

Go to **www.av2books.com**, and enter this book's unique code.

**BOOK CODE**

**P 3 2 6 1 7 5**

**AV² by Weigl** brings you media enhanced books that support active learning.

Published by AV² by Weigl
350 5th Avenue, 59th Floor
New York, NY 10118
Website: www.weigl.com    www.av2books.com

Library of Congress Cataloging-in-Publication Data

Amazing animals / edited by Jordan McGill.
    p. cm. -- (Learn to draw)
Includes index.
ISBN 978-1-61690-856-0 (hardcover : alk. paper) -- ISBN 978-1-61690-862-1 (pbk. : alk. paper) -- ISBN 978-1-61690-985-7 (online)
1. Animals in art--Juvenile literature. 2. Drawing--Technique--Juvenile literature. I. McGill, Jordan.
NC780.A46 2011
743.6--dc23

                        2011020309

Printed in the United States of America in North Mankato, Minnesota
1 2 3 4 5 6 7 8 9 0  15 14 13 12 11

062011
WEP290411

Project Coordinator: Jordan McGill
Art Director: Terry Paulhus

Every reasonable effort has been made to trace ownership and to obtain permission to reprint copyright material. The publishers would be pleased to have any errors or omissions brought to their attention so that they may be corrected in subsequent printings.

Weigl acknowledges Getty Images as its primary image supplier for this title.

# Contents

2 . . . . AV² Book Code

4 . . . . Why Draw?

5 . . . . Amazing Animals

6 . . . . Meet the Alligator

10 . . . . Meet the Dolphin

14 . . . . Meet the Elephant

18 . . . . Meet the Gorilla

22 . . . . Meet the Lion

26 . . . . Meet the Shark

30 . . . . Test Your Knowledge of Amazing Animals

31 . . . . Draw an Environment/ Glossary

32 . . . . Log on to av2books.com

6

10

14

18

22

26

# Why Draw?

**D**rawing is easier than you think. Look around you. The world is made of shapes and lines. By combining simple shapes and lines, anything can be drawn. An orange is just a circle with a few details added. A flower can be a circle with ovals drawn around it. An ice cream cone can be a triangle topped with a circle. Most anything, no matter how complicated, can be broken down into simple shapes.

oval

circle

circle

circle

triangle

Drawing helps people make sense of the world. It is a way to reduce an object to its simplest form, say our most personal feelings and thoughts, or show others objects from our **imagination**. Drawing an object can help you learn how it fits together and works.

**What shapes do you see in this car?**

It is fun to put the world onto a page, but it is also a good way to learn. Learning to draw even simple objects introduces the skills needed to fully express oneself visually. Drawing is an excellent form of **communication** and improves people's imagination.

Practice drawing your favorite animals in this book to learn the basic skills necessary to draw. You can use those skills to create your own drawings.

# Amazing Animals

**D**rawing the animals in this book is a great way to learn about the different parts and features that make these animals successful in their environment. As you draw each part of the animals in this book, consider how that part benefits the animal. Think about how the animal would survive without that feature.

Incredible animals that defy belief live in all parts of the world. These animals find everything they need to live in their environment. In nature, they live best without interference from humans. They have adapted to be very successful in their environments. Some animals, such as the shark, have lived successfully for millions of years.

# Meet the Alligator

Alligators belong to a group of animals called reptiles. Reptiles have hard, scaly skin all over their bodies. Snakes, lizards, and turtles are also reptiles.

Alligators spend part of their time on land and part of their time in rivers or lakes. They are expert swimmers. Alligators stay near the surface of the water so that they can breathe air.

**Eyes**
Alligators have good eyesight and can see well underwater. They have a clear eyelid that covers their eyes underwater. This allows them to see underwater without irritation.

**Nostrils**
**Nostrils** on top of the alligator's head let the animal breathe while it hides underwater.

**Jaws**
Alligators have very sharp teeth for catching and eating **prey**. Alligators eat only meat.

**Plates**
Tough, scaly skin protects the alligator from other animals.

**Tail**
An alligator pushes itself through the water with its strong tail. Sometimes, an alligator will use its tail to knock other animals down.

**Claws**
Alligators have five claws on each front foot and four claws on each back foot. They have webbing between their claws. This helps them swim.

# How to Draw an
# Alligator

**1** Start with a simple stick figure of the alligator. Use circles for the head and body, ovals for the feet, and lines for the limbs and tail.

**2** Now, join the two body circles together with a smooth, curved line. Also, draw the jaws and a small circle on the tip of the upper jaw. This will become the alligator's **snout**.

**3** Next, join the circles for the head and body with curved lines, and draw the tail around the tail line.

**4** In this step, draw the legs and tongue, as shown.

**5** Next, draw the webbed paws and a lump on the head, which is the eye on the other side.

**6** Draw the other eye and teeth. Also, draw scales on the body and tail using small curved lines.

**7** Draw lumps on the back and tail, and add checkered lines on the belly for scales.

**8** Erase the extra lines and the stick figure frame.

**9** Color the picture.

# Meet the Dolphin

Dolphins are friendly and smart animals that always seem to be smiling. They live in natural bodies of water around the world.

Many people confuse dolphins with fish. Dolphins are **marine mammals**. They breathe air just like humans. Every few minutes, a dolphin rises to the surface of the ocean to breathe through a blowhole on top of their head.

**Blowhole**
The blowhole is used for breathing. Dolphins keep the blowhole shut when underwater. They only open it to breathe.

**Melon**
The melon, located on the forehead, helps send underwater sounds.

**Beak**
Inside a dolphin's beak are teeth. A dolphin's teeth are cone-shaped with sharp points. They are used to grab and hold on to food.

**Dorsal Fin**
The dorsal fin helps keep
the dolphin balanced.

**Flippers**
Flippers are used to steer
the dolphin through water.

**Tail**
The tail moves up and down.
It helps the dolphin swim.

# How to Draw a Dolphin

**1** Start with a simple stick figure of the dolphin. Use circles for the body, ovals for the snout and head, and lines for the fins.

**2** Now, join the two body circles together with a smooth, curved line, in the shape of a curved teardrop.

**3** Next, join the head oval with the body circles using curved lines, and draw the tail fins.

**4** In this step, draw the dorsal fin and flippers.

**5** Next, draw the eye.

**6** Draw curved lines on the head and snout, as shown.

**7** Now, draw a curved line on the body and complete the head and fins.

**8** Erase the extra lines and the stick figure frame.

**9** Color the picture.

# Meet the Elephant

The elephant is the largest animal that lives on land. It has a huge, bulky body and a long nose called a trunk. Two curved tusks grow on either side of the trunk. Tusks are long, sharp teeth. They are made of a hard material called ivory.

**Tusks**
Sharp tusks are useful for digging up plants to eat.

**Trunk**
A trunk can make a loud noise like a trumpet to call other elephants. To drink, an elephant sucks up water with its trunk. Then, it sprays the water into its mouth.

**Legs**
Strong legs with wide feet support the elephant's body.

**Ears**
An elephant flaps its large ears to keep itself cool.

**Skin**
Thick skin protects the elephant from thorns and stinging insects. The wrinkles keep the elephant cool by trapping moisture in the folds.

# How to Draw an Elephant

① Start with a simple stick figure of the elephant. Use a circle for the body, ovals for the head and trunk, and lines for the limbs.

② Now, join the head oval and body circle with a smooth, curved line. Also, draw the trunk with curved lines, as shown.

**3** Next, draw the legs.

**4** In this step, draw the eyes and tail.

**5** Next, draw the ears.

**6** Now, draw the tusks and nails.

**7** Draw curved lines on the head, body, and ears for the wrinkles. Also, draw hair on the tail.

**8** Erase the extra lines and the stick figure frame.

**9** Color the picture.

# Meet the Gorilla

Gorillas are big, strong, intelligent animals. They live in the forests of West and Central Africa.

Most people think that gorillas are scary animals. Gorillas are very calm, peaceful, and kind. These big, fearsome-looking animals are **herbivores**.

Gorillas are the largest members of the great ape family.

**Face**
Gorillas have no hair on their face. Each gorilla has its own unique facial features.

**Nose**
Gorillas have distinct noses. Researchers can tell one gorilla from another by the shape of its nose.

**Hands**
Gorilla hands have five fingers and an **opposable** thumb. Gorillas use their hands to eat. They mostly eat plants.

**Head Crest**
Gorillas have a bulging forehead called a crest.

**Chest**
Their wide chest makes gorillas appear huge. Gorillas beat their chest when they are excited, angry, or frightened.

**Feet**
Gorilla feet have five toes and an opposable toe.

19

# How to Draw a Gorilla

1. Start with a simple stick figure of the gorilla. Use ovals for the head, hands, feet, and body. Use lines for the limbs.

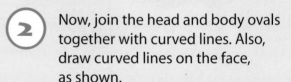

2. Now, join the head and body ovals together with curved lines. Also, draw curved lines on the face, as shown.

**3** Next, draw the arms and legs.

**4** In this step, draw the hands and feet.

**5** Next, draw the nose, mouth, ear, and nails.

**6** Now, draw the eyes.

**7** Draw hair on the head, body, and limbs.

**8** Erase the extra lines and the stick figure frame.

**9** Color the picture.

# Meet the Lion

A lion is a large animal with four strong legs and sharp teeth. A female lion is called a lioness. Lions are **mammals**, which are animals that feed their babies milk and have hair or fur on their bodies.

Lions belong to the same family as pet cats, but a person could not keep a mighty lion as a pet. It is one of the fiercest **predators** on Earth.

**Eyes**
A lion's large eyes help it to see well at night.

**Back Claws**
Lions' back paws have four sharp claws. A lion's claws can be three inches (7.6 cm) long.

**Mane**
A mane is the thick hair that covers much of a lion's head and upper body. The shaggy mane protects the lion's neck against attacks by other lions.

**Jaws**
Lions' powerful jaws and long, pointed teeth are used for killing other animals. A lion may eat 70 pounds (32 kg) of meat in one meal. That is the same as eating 280 large hamburgers.

**Paws**
A lion's huge paws have soft pads that help the animal move quietly while hunting.

# How to Draw a Lion

**1** Start with a simple stick figure of the lion. Use circles for the head and body, ovals for the snout and feet, and lines for the limbs and tail.

**2** Now, join the two body circles together with a smooth, curved line. Also, draw a large circle around the head. This will become the lion's mane.

24

**3** Next, draw the ears and mouth.

**4** In this step, draw the legs, as shown.

**5** Next, draw the tail and paws.

**6** Now, draw the eyes, nose, whiskers, and nails.

**7** Draw the mane and hair around the head, body, and tail.

**8** Erase the extra lines and the stick figure frame.

**9** Color the picture.

# Meet the Shark

**Snout**
A shark's snout is used to smell, but not to breathe. The great white shark can smell one drop of blood in 25 gallons (95 liters) of water.

Great white sharks are large, meat-eating fish. They are the most dangerous of all sharks.

The great white shark's skin is covered with a layer of tiny teeth called denticles. These denticles make the shark's skin feel like sandpaper.

**Teeth**
Sharks have sharp teeth and huge jaws. Great white sharks tear their food into mouth-sized pieces that they swallow whole.

**Pectoral Fins**
Pectoral fins on both sides of a shark's body control direction of movement.

**Gill Slits**
Gills are used for breathing.

**Dorsal Fin**
The dorsal fin helps the shark keep its balance.

**Tail**
Great white sharks have a tail shaped like a moon.

# How to Draw a Shark

**1** Start by drawing a stick figure of the shark. Use circles for the head and body, and lines for the fins.

**2** Now, join the two body circles together with smooth, curved lines starting from tip of the central line and ending before the tail fin.

**3** Now, draw the dorsal and tail fins and one of the pectoral fins.

**4** In this step, draw the other pectoral fin, as shown.

**5** Next, draw the eye, nostrils, and mouth.

**6** Now, draw the teeth. Also, draw the small fins on the shark's underside.

**7** Draw curved lines on the body, which will become the gill slits.

**8** Erase the extra lines and the stick figure frame.

**9** Color the picture.

# Test Your Knowledge of Amazing Animals

**1.** Alligators belong to what group of animals?

Answer: Reptiles

**2.**

Are dolphins fish?

Answer: No. Dolphins are marine mammals.

**3.**

What material are an elephant's tusks made of?

Answer: Ivory

**4.**

What do gorillas mostly eat?

Answer: Plants

**5.**

How large are lions' claws?

Answer: A lion's claws can be three inches (7.6 cm) long.

**6.**

What is a shark's snout used for?

Answer: To smell

Want to learn more? Log on to av2books.com to access more content.

# Draw an Environment

**Materials**
Large white poster board
Internet connection or library
Pencils and crayons or markers
Glue or tape

**Steps**
1. Complete one of the animal drawings in this book. Cut out the drawing.
2. Using this book, the internet, and a library, find out about your animal and the environment in which it lives.
3. Think about what the animal might see and hear in its environment. What does its environment look like? What sorts of trees are there? Is there water? What does the landscape look like? Are there other animals in its environment? What in the animal's environment is essential to its survival? What other important features might you find in the animal's environment?
4. On the large white poster board, draw an environment for your animal. Be sure to place all the features you noted in step 3.
5. Place the cutout animal in its environment with glue or tape. Color the animal's environment to complete the activity.

# Glossary

**communication:** the sending and receiving of information

**herbivores:** animals that eat plants

**imagination:** the ability to form new creative ideas or images

**mammals:** animals that have fur, make milk, and are born live

**marine mammals:** warm-blooded animals that live in water

**nostrils:** openings on the nose that admit air and scents

**opposable:** the ability to place the first finger and the thumb together to grasp things

**predators:** animals that hunt other animals for food

**prey:** an animal that is hunted for food

**snout:** the projecting nose and mouth of an animal

# Log on to www.av2books.com

AV² by Weigl brings you media enhanced books that support active learning. Go to www.av2books.com, and enter the special code found on page 2 of this book. You will gain access to enriched and enhanced content that supplements and complements this book. Content includes video, audio, web links, quizzes, a slide show, and activities.

**Audio**
Listen to sections of the book read aloud.

**Video**
Watch informative video clips.

**Embedded Weblinks**
Gain additional information for research.

**Try This!**
Complete activities and hands-on experiments.

# WHAT'S ONLINE?

|  Try This! |  Embedded Weblinks |  Video | EXTRA FEATURES |
|---|---|---|---|
| Complete an interactive drawing tutorial for each of the six amazing animals in the book. | Learn more about each of the six amazing animals in the book. | Watch a video about amazing animals. |  **Audio** Listen to sections of the book read aloud. |
| | | |  **Key Words** Study vocabulary, and complete a matching word activity. |
| | | |  **Slide Show** View images and captions, and prepare a presentation. |
| | | |  **Quizzes** Test your knowledge. |

**AV² was built to bridge the gap between print and digital. We encourage you to tell us what you like and what you want to see in the future.**

## Sign up to be an AV² Ambassador at www.av2books.com/ambassador.